Katie
LET'S CELEBRATE YOUR STORY

HERE I GO!

A TRAVEL JOURNAL

sourcebooks
eXplore

TO TODD AND MICHELLE.
I'LL ALWAYS SQUEEZE INTO THE
BACKSEAT WITH YOU FOR AN ADVENTURE.

NIKLAS'S ART.
AGE 6

Published by Sourcebooks eXplore, an imprint of Sourcebooks Kids
P.O. Box 4410, Naperville, Illinois 60567–4410
(630) 961-3900
sourcebookskids.com

Source of Production: Versa Press, East Peoria, Illinois, USA
Date of Production: March 2020
Run Number: 5018345

Printed and bound in the United States of America.
VP 10 9 8 7 6 5 4 3 2 1

READY FOR ADVENTURE

ON THE FIRST DAY of family vacation, I clutched a thick yellow notebook in my hands. I sat quietly at the airport with trail mix, a toothbrush, and an extra change of clothes in my backpack. I was waiting for our flight, but I was hoping for inspiration—the life-changing spark a friend told me every great travel journalist began with.

"You have to record everything," my friend had insisted. Gosh, that notebook felt thick and heavy in my hands. I cracked it open and wrote the first words: *We are sitting at the Salt Lake City airport.* I didn't really know what else to write—my family and I hadn't done anything yet. People were rushing by. Others just waited in chairs, in lines.

My mom tapped my shoulder. "We'd better go to the bathroom before it's time to board the plane, Katie." I nodded and stuffed the notebook in my backpack, figuring I'd write more later.

A couple weeks passed and we were back home, unpacking dirty clothes and souvenirs. I was pulling out ticket stubs, postcards, and creased brochures that were buried everywhere. Then I unearthed my notebook—still with just one sentence written in it.

Over the years I've learned that the trickiest part of journaling is putting pen to paper, especially when I don't know where to start. I've also discovered I'm not alone in my struggles. Many of us begin listing details other people tell us are important: our location, what we're eating, what the weather looks like. This data can be a useful element of our story, but it can't stand on its own.

To make a great travel journal, you need to capture experiences in ways that remind you of not only *what* happened, but *how* those events made you feel. When you pick up your pen, note what interests you. Stories worth recording are the ones you can't stop talking about at the end of the day. They're the moments you dream about or repeat to your friends.

Think of this book as a map guiding you through those stories, with prompts to help you think about your trip from different angles. Some pages will make you reflect and laugh, while others will challenge you to describe moments in unique, memorable ways. You decide where this map will take you. To spur you along the trail, here are seven guideposts that will help you get the most from your journal.

I. START ON ANY PAGE

Whenever you use this journal, flip to the prompt page that inspires you. Day-at-a-glance stories go on pages that begin with phrases like "Around Here" or "Today I." Other pages offer you an opportunity to expand on individual moments or explore the broader scope of your trip. Make sure to record the date, then write as much or as little as you want, using as many pages as you need. Some days carry more weight than others, so you don't have to treat them equally.

2. WELCOME IMPERFECTION

The best journal entries are never flawless. Make up words, tear out pages, or roll up this book and stuff it in your pocket. A great journal is one that gets used. I cross out words, use awkward grammar, misspell words, and get food crumbs on my pages all the time—and I'm an adult! One time I had a spread of blank prompts, ones that I didn't feel like doing, so I just glued them together and kept going.

3. COLLECT MEMENTOS

Souvenirs bring visual excitement to embellish your entries. I always carry a zip pouch with scissors and double-sided tape so I can quickly combine my words with objects like ticket stubs, stickers, menus, brochures, postcards, candy wrappers, receipts, or even logos I cut from shopping bags. Photographs are entirely optional.

4. DOODLE AND DECORATE

This journal is a home for words, but it's also a place to play! These experiments are a few of my favorites. Mark any you'd like to try.

☐ MAKE IT COLORFUL

Use different media such as pens, pencils, crayons, or watercolors. Glue in plants or other objects you find in nature.

☐ WRITE IN DIFFERENT DIRECTIONS

Rotate the book, then compose sideways or in a circle. Make words go backward or up and down.

☐ EMPHASIZE IMPORTANT WORDS AND IDEAS

Use a highlighter. Print in all caps or bubble letters. Color in every o and a. Trace your penmanship with a second color. Draw boxes and underlines.

☐ MAKE A CARTOON

Tell wordless stories through sketches.

☐ DECORATE YOUR PAGE

Draw arrows, speech bubbles, zigzags, signs, or swirly borders.

☐ EMPLOY CONTRAST

Make a page as colorful as you can, then make your next one black and white.

What other techniques could you play with?

Come join me online for exclusive examples from my own travel diaries and cool tricks you can try at:

KATIECLEMONS.COM/A/BE7R

5. ASSEMBLE MATERIALS

While access to a variety of scrapbooking products is fun, I've learned that the most creative journals can be crafted with less. With only a pen or pencil and some tape or glue you can build a cool journal by personalizing it with "found" stuff. You can always add more when you return home.

List supplies you want to carry with this journal:

☐

☐

☐

☐

☐

☐

6. FIND AN ADULT TO HELP

You might be so busy having fun on this vacation that you forget to journal. That's okay! If you'd like, ask an adult who is accompanying you to help you:

☐ set aside time to write

☐ discover cool mementos to add to your pages

☐ remember where you put this book

☐ understand new words

☐ recollect important names and information

Who are you asking? Why?

_____

_____

This adult said

☐ yes ☐ no ☐ I'll think about it

7. CLAIM THIS JOURNAL

Look at that—you've already set the tone and written more than I did at the Salt Lake City airport. You're officially a travel journaler. Yahoo! So hang onto your pen, flip the page, and start telling your tale. Bon voyage. Have fun, and... Let's celebrate your story!

P.S. Want to share your ideas with me? Email **howdy@katieclemons.com** (I answer all my mail) or join me on social media **@katierclemons**, **#katieclemonsjournals**, and **#hereigo**.

♡ Katie

HERE'S A PHOTOGRAPH
OR DRAWING OF
ME AND
MY GEAR

HERE I GO!

MY FULL NAME IS

_____

ON THIS ADVENTURE, I WANT EVERYONE TO CALL ME

_____

I'M TAKING A TRIP TO

_____

FOR _____ DAYS.

START DATE

_____

END DATE

_____

IMPORTANT DATE

_____

I'M HEADING TO

_____ !

HERE'S WHAT I ALREADY KNOW ABOUT THE PLACE

_____

_____

I'M REALLY EXCITED TO

_____

I'M CURIOUS ABOUT

_____

I FEEL A LITTLE HESITANT ABOUT

_____

I'VE TAKEN THIS ADVENTURE BEFORE. ☐ YES ☐ NO

MY JOURNAL
GUIDELINES

1. IS MY JOURNAL TOP SECRET OR CAN ANYONE ELSE LOOK INSIDE? _____

2. IF SOMEONE FINDS THIS JOURNAL, THEY SHOULD

☐ EMAIL OR TEXT ME (OR AN ADULT I TRUST) AT

_____

☐ MAIL IT TO MY HOME ADDRESS

_____

_____

☐ DROP IT OFF AT _____

☐ COMPLETE IT

☐ DESTROY IT

☐ SHARE PAGES ONLINE #HEREIGO

☐ SELL IT TO A TRAVEL MAGAZINE FOR $_____

☐ TURN IT INTO A _____ MOVIE

☐ DONATE IT TO THE _____ MUSEUM

3. DO I HAVE TO ANSWER PROMPTS IN NUMERICAL ORDER? ☐ YES ☐ NO

4. MY TOP FOCUS(ES) IN THIS JOURNAL WILL BE TO

☐ EXPRESS MY THOUGHTS

☐ USE PERFECT GRAMMAR

☐ CAPTURE MEMORIES

☐ RECORD NEW DISCOVERIES

☐ PLAY AND HAVE FUN

☐ DOCUMENT EVERY SECOND OF MY JOURNEY

☐ _____

☐ _____

5. WHAT COULD I DO IF I NEED MORE SPACE TO WRITE?

6. DO I NEED TO ENCLOSE PHOTOGRAPHS? ☐ YES ☐ NO

7. DO I HAVE TO USE EVERY PAGE OF MY JOURNAL TO RECORD MY ADVENTURE? ☐ YES ☐ NO

8. SHOULD I TRY TO COMPLETE THIS JOURNAL ON MY TRIP OR WHEN I GET BACK HOME AND CAN REFLECT?

9. WILL I WANT TO KEEP ADDITIONAL VOLUMES OF THIS JOURNAL ON FUTURE ADVENTURES?

☐ YES ☐ NO

VOLUME 1: _____

VOLUME 2: _____

VOLUME 3: _____

10. ARE THERE OTHER GUIDELINES I SHOULD ESTABLISH BEFORE I BEGIN?

I'M ADVENTURING WITH THESE PEOPLE

I'M EXCITED TO BE HERE WITH THEM BECAUSE

I THINK THEY'LL MAKE ME LAUGH WHEN

TYPES OF TRANSPORTATION
I PLAN ON USING

☐ FEET ☐ CANOE OR SMALL BOAT ☐ SHIP

☐ BUS ☐ CAR ☐ PLANE

☐ TRAIN ☐ HELICOPTER ☐ RV

☐ CAMEL-BACK ☐ HORSEBACK ☐ PIGGYBACK

☐ FERRY ☐ MOTORCYCLE ☐ RICKSHAW

☐ BUGGY ☐ FLYING CAR ☐ SKIS

☐ BIKE ☐ TRUCK

☐ SUBWAY ☐ STREETCAR/TRAM

☐ _____

☐ _____

HERE'S THE ROUTE I'M TAKING

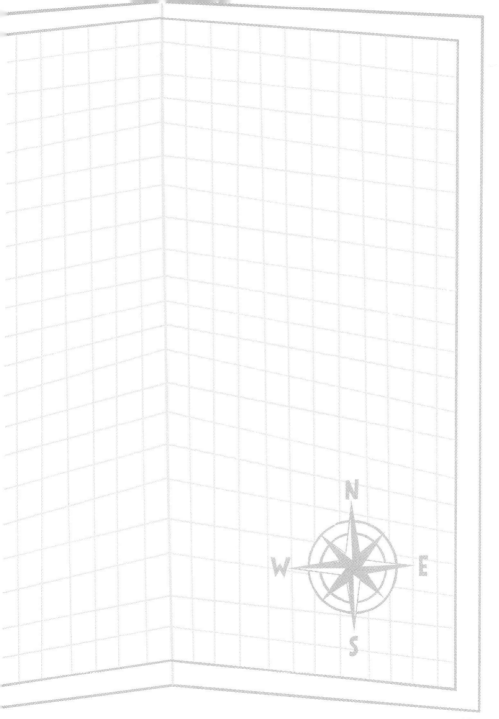

THINGS I CARRY

THIS
FAVORITE SHIRT

THESE GO-TO SHOES

THIS
SNACK

THIS HAT

THIS TOOTHBRUSH

THIS BAG

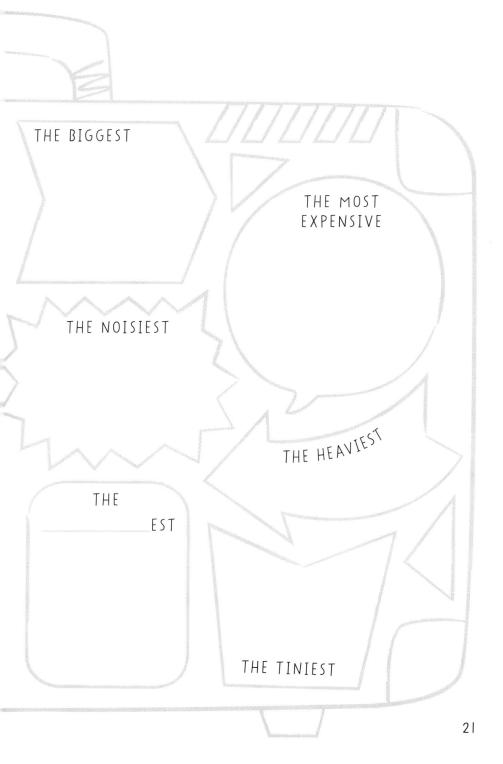

THE BIGGEST

THE MOST EXPENSIVE

THE NOISIEST

THE HEAVIEST

THE _____EST

THE TINIEST

21

TODAY I AM _____ ING
AT _____ !

TODAY'S TEMPERATURE

IT'S A ☆☆☆☆☆ STAR

DAY BECAUSE

1. _____

_____

2. _____

_____

3. _____

_____

I WATCH

I TOUCH

I TRY

I'M GRATEFUL FOR

1.

2.

3.

I'M HAPPY BECAUSE

I LEARNED THAT

I GIVE TODAY

I WONDER WHAT WOULD HAPPEN IF

THIS IS MY FACE WHEN I'M

GOOFY

OVERJOYED

SLEEPY

INTRIGUED

BORED

CRANKY

DATE

SURPRISED THAT

CHILL

BURSTING INTO SONG

GRATEFUL

LOOKING
FORWARD TO

HERE'S ME IN MY PAJAMAS

MOST NIGHTS, I

☐ STAY UP LATE   ☐ WAKE UP CRABBY

☐ KICK OFF MY BLANKET   ☐ WAKE UP EARLY

☐ DREAM   ☐ BARELY SLEEP

☐ SLEEP IN   ☐ FEEL HOT

☐ SLEEP LIKE A ROCK   ☐ DROOL

☐ SNORE   ☐ GRIND MY TEETH

☐ SLEEPWALK   ☐ LOSE MY PILLOW

☐ TALK IN MY SLEEP   ☐ _____

☐ GET COLD   ☐ _____

I GO TO SLEEP AT   AND WAKE UP AT

SOMETIMES I CAN'T SLEEP BECAUSE I'M THINKING

ABOUT _____

_____

_____

_____

31

HERE'S MY BED

I'M SLEEPING IN A

☐ TENT

☐ HOTEL ROOM

☐ HOUSE

☐ IGLOO

☐ YURT

☐ APARTMENT

☐ CABIN

☐ BOAT

☐ CAMPER

☐ VEHICLE

☐ SLEEPING BAG UNDER THE STARS

☐ _____

I LIKE TO SLEEP WITH _____

BECAUSE _____

LYING HERE,

DATE

I HEAR

I SMELL

I SEE

I WONDER

33

MY DAY BY THE HOUR

6:00

7:00

8:00

9:00

10:00

11:00

NOON

1:00

2:00

3:00

4:00

5:00

6:00

7:00

8:00

9:00

10:00

11:00

TODAY

THIS MADE ME
REALLY HAPPY

THIS INSPIRED
OR INTRIGUED ME

THIS MADE
ME LOL

THIS WAS
REALLY FUN

LOL

IT'S GOOD TO BE BORED SOMETIMES BECAUSE THAT'S WHEN I

A COLOR HUNT

PURPLE

BLUE

GREEN

DRAW OR JOT DOWN DISCOVERIES

LOOK BIG. LOOK SMALL. THINK MAN-MADE.
THINK NATURE. LOOK ABOVE AND BELOW.

YELLOW

ORANGE

RED

WHITE

GRAY

BLACK

BROWN

A COLOR I LOVE

A COLOR I DON'T LIKE

HERE'S ME IN THE MORNING

I WOKE UP TODAY AT **BECAUSE**

_____

_____

☐ YIPPEE! I'M UP AND READY TO ROLL.

☐ WHERE'S MY BED?

☐ I'M SO HUNGRY.

☐ I HAVE NO IDEA WHAT TO EXPECT TODAY.

☐ I HOPE I GET TO _____

DATE

HERE'S ME BEFORE BED

I'M GOING TO BED AT TONIGHT,

AFTER A _____ DAY

FULL OF _____

☐ WAIT! I WANT TO KEEP GOING!

☐ WHERE'S MY BED?

☐ I'M SO HUNGRY.

☐ I'M READY TO DREAM ABOUT _____

☐ I'M GLAD I GOT TO _____

I ESTIMATE THE NUMBER OF

SHOES I PACKED

DIRTY PAIRS OF UNDERWEAR I'LL TAKE HOME

DOLLARS I'VE SPENT

INSECT BITES ON MY BODY

BOTTLES OF _____ I'M CONSUMING

TIMES I'VE SAID, "_____!"

MINUTES I'VE THOUGHT, "I'M SO BORED"

_____

_____

_____

I WANT TO HANG ONTO THIS

DATE

IT'S A

☐ TICKET STUB

☐ BUSINESS CARD

☐ RECEIPT

☐ POSTCARD

☐ BROCHURE CLIPPING

☐ LIST OR NOTE FROM MY POCKET

☐ PHOTO OR PICTURE

☐ WRAPPER OR NAPKIN

☐ _____

I'M ADDING IT TO MY JOURNAL BECAUSE

_____

_____

WHERE I WALK

PATTERNS AND TEXTURES UNDER MY FEET

TODAY

ON THE ITINERARY

ON MY FEET

IN MY HANDS

IN MY STOMACH

I HAVE TO RECORD THIS BEFORE I FORGET!

DATE

I GIVE IT ☆☆☆☆☆ STARS!

MY DAY IN
DOODLES

TODAY'S CHECKLIST

- ☐ TRY SOMETHING I'VE NEVER DONE
- ☐ LAUGH
- ☐ BE HELPFUL
- ☐ SAY THANK YOU
- ☐ EAT A NEW FOOD OR SOMETHING I DON'T NORMALLY LIKE
- ☐ HAVE FUN
- ☐ _____
- ☐ _____

HERE'S MY STORY

IN MY BAG

I'M GLAD I BROUGHT

I DIDN'T NEED TO BRING

I'M TAKING HOME

I THINK I MISPLACED

A SCENT HUNT

FRAGRANT
(FOR EXAMPLE, FLORALS AND PERFUMES)

FRUITY
(E.G. ALL NON-CITRUS FRUITS)

CITRUS
(E.G. LEMON, LIME, ORANGE)

WOODY + RESINOUS
(E.G. PINE, FRESH-CUT GRASS)

MINTY + PEPPERMINT
(E.G. EUCALYPTUS, CAMPHOR)

CHEMICAL
(E.G. AMMONIA, BLEACH)

DECAYED
(E.G. ROTTING MEAT, SOUR MILK)

SWEET
(E.G. VANILLA, CHOCOLATE, CARAMEL)

PUNGENT
E.G. BLUE CHEESE, CIGAR SMOKE)

TOASTED + NUTTY
(E.G. POPCORN, PEANUT BUTTER, ALMONDS)

MY NOSE FINDS THESE SMELLS AROUND HERE

FRAGRANT

FRUITY

CITRUS

WOODY + RESINOUS

CHEMICAL

THE SCENT HUNT CONTINUES

SWEET

MINTY + PEPPERMINT

TOASTED + NUTTY

PUNGENT

DECAYED

OF ALL THE SCENTS I'M EXPERIENCING,
I REALLY WANT TO REMEMBER THE
SMELL OF _____
BECAUSE _____
_____
_____
_____

WHEN I SMELLED IT, HERE'S WHAT I WAS
DOING _____
_____
_____
_____

HERE'S HOW I WAS FEELING
_____
_____
_____

STRONG
SMELL

SCENT-O-METER

AROUND HERE

HERE'S WHAT WAS ON TODAY'S SCHEDULE

HERE'S WHAT WAS NOT ON THE SCHEDULE

☐ IT HAPPENED ANYWAY

HERE'S HOW MY DAY STARTED

AND HERE'S HOW IT ENDED

I REALLY ENJOYED TODAY BECAUSE

I'M DISCOVERING COOL THINGS!

PEOPLE MAKING THIS EXPERIENCE GREAT FOR ME INCLUDE

☐ I HAVE TOLD THOSE PEOPLE, "THANKS!"

THIS FELT
SCARY AT FIRST

I ALMOST DIDN'T DO IT. ☐ TRUE ☐ FALSE

IN THE END, I'M GLAD I DID IT. ☐ TRUE ☐ FALSE

HERE'S THE STORY

THE EXPERIENCE MADE ME FEEL _____

THE BEST PART WAS _____

THE TOUGHEST PART WAS _____

I'D DO IT AGAIN. ☐ TRUE ☐ FALSE

I GIVE IT ☆☆☆☆☆ STARS!

AROUND HERE,
I HEAR FOLKS SAY

I KEEP SAYING

AROUND HERE, I SEE

ABOVE ME

AT EYE LEVEL WITH ME

BELOW ME

70

DATE

BIGGER
THAN
ME

SMALLER THAN ME

SAME SIZE AS ME

71

WITHOUT THIS TRIP, I NEVER WOULD'VE KNOWN

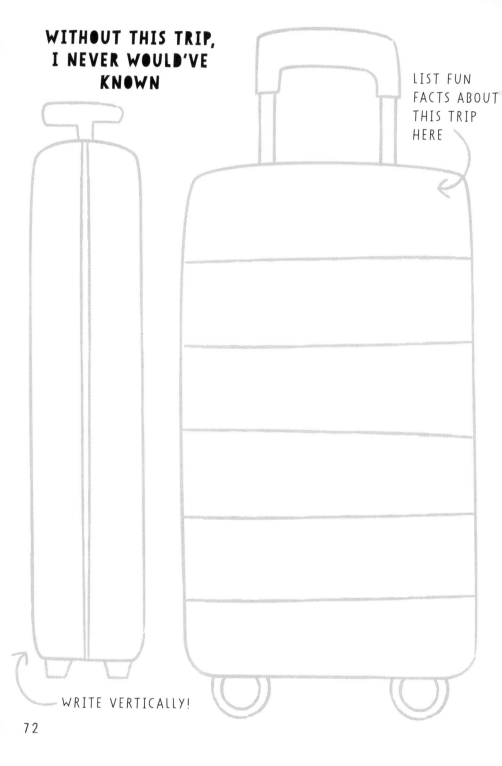

LIST FUN FACTS ABOUT THIS TRIP HERE

WRITE VERTICALLY!

I LEARNED

DATE

MY TRIP THEME SONG

SHH... PACK TRIP SECRETS IN HERE!

A BREAKFAST I OFTEN EAT HERE

A BREAKFAST I TYPICALLY HAVE BACK HOME

A BEVERAGE I USUALLY DRINK HERE

A DRINK I NORMALLY HAVE BACK HOME

A SNACK I LOVED TRYING HERE

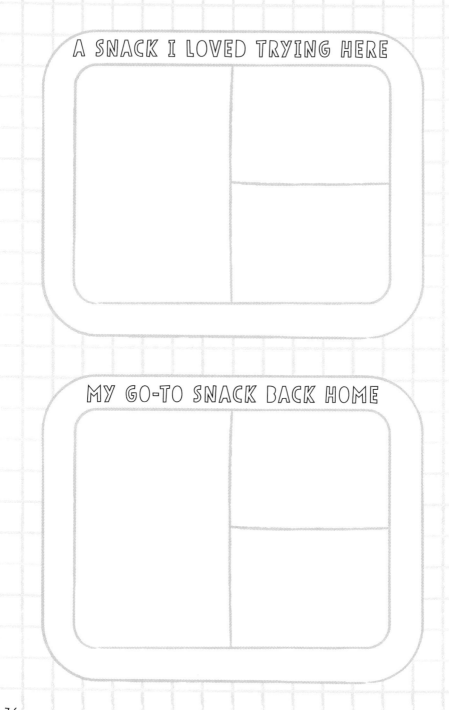

MY GO-TO SNACK BACK HOME

A DELICIOUS DINNER I HAD HERE

A TASTY DINNER I ENJOY BACK HOME

A TEXTURE HUNT

ROUGH

SPIKY

SMOOTH

FURRY

STICKY

CRUMBLY

LOOK BIG. LOOK SMALL. THINK MAN-MADE. THINK NATURE. SEE ABOVE AND BELOW.

DATE

FLAKY

MATTE

SHINY

BEAUTIFUL

SOFT

STRANGE

TODAY I AM _____ ING
AT _____ !

TODAY'S TEMPERATURE

IT'S A _____

DAY BECAUSE

1. _____
   _____

2. _____
   _____

3. _____
   _____

I SEE

I TRY

I EAT

80

I'M GRATEFUL FOR

1.

2.

3.

I'M CHUCKLING BECAUSE

I'M SMILING BECAUSE

I GIVE TODAY ☆☆☆☆☆ STARS!

RETRACING MY STEPS TODAY

WAKE UP

SOUVENIRS
I'M TAKING HOME

I THINK IT'S INTERESTING THAT

I'M HAVING SO MUCH FUN TODAY!

☐ TRUE ☐ FALSE

BECAUSE _____

_____

ON A SCALE OF 1-5, I FEEL

EXCITED 1 2 3 4 5

RESTED 1 2 3 4 5

CURIOUS 1 2 3 4 5

HERE'S WHY _____

_____

_____

_____

HERE'S A DRAWING OR KEEPSAKE

THAT CAPTURES MY ☆☆☆☆☆ DAY

PLANTS AROUND HERE

THE LANDSCAPE
HAS A LOT OF

LOOKING UP,
I SEE

AT EYE LEVEL,
I SEE

ON THE GROUND,
I SEE

THESE PLANTS ☐ COULD ☐ COULDN'T
GROW BACK HOME BECAUSE

A PLANT HUNT

FOR SIX DIFFERENT SPECIMENS

A PLANT SAMPLE

THIS PLANT IS CALLED

(MAKE UP A NAME IF YOU DON'T KNOW!)

WHEN I LEAN IN TO EXAMINE IT, I SEE

WHEN I STEP BACK TO LOOK AT THE WHOLE PLANT, I SEE

I HAVE A PART OF THE PLANT IN
MY HAND. HERE'S WHERE I'M

☐ MAKING A RUBBING WITH A PENCIL OR CRAYON
☐ TRACING IT   ☐ PRESSING IT IN THESE PAGES

ITS COLORS ARE

ITS TEXTURES FEEL

ITS PATTERNS AND SHAPES ARE

I THINK THIS PLANT THRIVES WHEN

I CHOSE TO INCLUDE INFORMATION ABOUT THIS
PLANT IN MY JOURNAL BECAUSE

HERE'S ME DOING MY THING

AROUND HERE, I HEAR

**THIS IS ME
HURRYING SOMEWHERE**

**THIS IS ME
TAKING MY TIME**

94

THIS IS ME
GETTING CREATIVE

THIS IS ME ACTING
RESOURCEFUL

HERE'S A PICTURE OF ME ENJOYING

MY TRIP IN A SOUVENIR SNOW GLOBE

AROUND HERE

TODAY'S THEME
SONG COULD BE

THIS IS ME RIGHT NOW

I'M FEELING REALLY _____ BECAUSE

SO FAR ON THIS ADVENTURE, I HAVE

- ☐ SEEN SOMEONE FAMOUS
- ☐ STOOD IN A LINE
- ☐ RECEIVED A HUG FROM SOMEONE SPECIAL
- ☐ OBSERVED SOMETHING NEW
- ☐ LAUGHED UNTIL MY BELLY ACHED
- ☐ EXPERIENCED SOMETHING REALLY FUN

HERE'S ONE OF THOSE STORIES

SUPER
AWESOME

AWESOMETER

I THINK I HAVE A NEW UNDERSTANDING OF

I'M STILL LOOKING FORWARD TO

1.

2.

3.

THINGS I ENJOY HERE

INTERESTING FACT

MAN-MADE THING

PIECE OF NATURE

WEATHER

LOCAL HISTORY

WAY PEOPLE CARE FOR THE EARTH

WAY PEOPLE CARE FOR EACH OTHER

A SHAPE HUNT

FIND THESE SHAPES IN EVERYDAY OBJECTS, NATURE, AND
MAN-MADE CREATIONS, THEN RECORD EACH DISCOVERY.

LOOK BIG. LOOK SMALL. SEE ABOVE AND BELOW.

AROUND HERE TODAY

I SEE

I TRY

I HEAR

I TASTE

DATE

I FORGET

I WONDER

I REALLY WANT
TO REMEMBER

IT'S A 👍/👎 DAY.

105

AROUND HERE,
A LOT OF PEOPLE

WEAR

SAY

CARRY

ENJOY

I LIKE BEING THE SAME AS EVERYONE WHEN

_____

_____

AROUND HERE, I

WEAR

SAY

CARRY

ENJOY

I LIKE BEING UNIQUE WHEN

WEATHER AROUND HERE

I NEED TO WEAR ⎯⎯⎯⎯⎯⎯⎯⎯⎯⎯⎯⎯⎯⎯⎯⎯⎯⎯⎯

I DON'T NEED TO WEAR ⎯⎯⎯⎯⎯⎯⎯⎯⎯⎯⎯⎯⎯⎯⎯

ON MY FEET ⎯⎯⎯⎯⎯⎯⎯⎯⎯⎯⎯⎯⎯⎯⎯⎯⎯⎯⎯⎯⎯⎯⎯

ON MY HEAD ⎯⎯⎯⎯⎯⎯⎯⎯⎯⎯⎯⎯⎯⎯⎯⎯⎯⎯⎯⎯⎯⎯⎯

I ☐ DO / ☐ DO NOT ENJOY IT BECAUSE

⎯⎯⎯⎯⎯⎯⎯⎯⎯⎯⎯⎯⎯⎯⎯⎯⎯⎯⎯⎯⎯⎯⎯⎯⎯⎯⎯⎯⎯⎯⎯

⎯⎯⎯⎯⎯⎯⎯⎯⎯⎯⎯⎯⎯⎯⎯⎯⎯⎯⎯⎯⎯⎯⎯⎯⎯⎯⎯⎯⎯⎯⎯

☐ I SAW SNOW!

☐ I GOT SUNBURNED.

☐ I GOT REALLY WET.

☐ MY _____ ALMOST BLEW AWAY.

☐ I CAN'T STOP SWEATING/SHIVERING.

☐ I'M ALWAYS LOOKING FOR SHADY/SUNNY SPOTS.

☐ IT'S MORE/LESS HUMID THAN HOME.

☐ _____

IT'S CURRENTLY _____ DEGREES,

AND THE SKY LOOKS LIKE

COMPARED TO HOME, IT'S _____ HERE.

I GIVE THIS WEATHER 👍 / 👎 BECAUSE

AROUND HERE TODAY

IN THREE SENTENCES

1. ....

2. ....

3. ....

IN THREE DOODLES

IN THREE EMOJIS

IN THREE COLORS

1. ....

2. ....

3. ....

IN THREE SOUNDS

1. ....

2. ....

3. ....

IN THREE WORDS

1. ....

2. ....

3. ....

SUPER
AWESOME

AWESOMETER

HERE'S THE PERFECT SOUVENIR T-SHIRT OF MY TRIP

REASONS I LOVE IT HERE

1. _____

2. _____

3. _____

4. _____

5. _____

I THINK ABOUT HOME WHENEVER

_____

_____

_____

_____

_____

_____

I TRIED SOMETHING NEW!

HERE'S THE WHOLE STORY

NEW THINGS

I ATE

I THINK IT'S 👍 / 👎

I TRIED

I THINK IT'S 👍 / 👎

I SAW

I THINK IT'S 👍 / 👎

HERE'S ME WRITING IN THIS JOURNAL

WHEN I WRITE, I'M USUALLY SITTING IN

I OFTEN WRITE BEFORE _____

AND AFTER _____

AROUND ME

I HEAR

I SEE

I SMELL

WHEN I FINISH THIS PAGE, I'M GOING TO

I'M EXCITED TO LOOK BACK AT MY JOURNAL ONE DAY
BECAUSE

WILDLIFE AROUND HERE

I SEE A LOT OF

THEY EAT A LOT OF

I LIKE WATCHING HOW THEY

I ALSO SEE A LOT OF

THEY EAT A LOT OF

I LIKE WATCHING HOW THEY

I THINK LIFE HERE IS ☐ EASIER ☐ MORE DIFFICULT
THAN IT IS FOR ANIMALS BACK HOME BECAUSE

TASTES AROUND HERE

SWEET

SOUR

SALTY

BITTER

NEW TO ME

DELICIOUS

UNAPPEALING

TYPICAL FOR THIS REGION

I LOVE THIS SONG

I THINK THESE ARE THE LYRICS

ONE LAST THING TO HANG ON TO

IT'S A

- ☐ TICKET STUB
- ☐ BUSINESS CARD
- ☐ RECEIPT
- ☐ POSTCARD
- ☐ BROCHURE CLIPPING

- ☐ LIST OR NOTE FROM MY POCKET
- ☐ PHOTO OR PICTURE
- ☐ WRAPPER OR NAPKIN
- ☐ _____

I'M ADDING IT TO MY JOURNAL BECAUSE

_____

_____

TODAY I'M

_____ !

MY FAVORITE THING ABOUT TODAY IS

HIGHLIGHTS OF MY DAY

1.

2.

3.

4.

5.

IT'S A ☆☆☆☆☆ STAR DAY!

GREETINGS FROM

IMAGINE MAILING THIS POSTCARD TO SOMEONE BACK HOME!

WRITE YOUR STORY ON THE FIRST SIDE. THEN USE THE OTHER SIDE TO DRAW A PICTURE OF WHERE YOU ARE, SOMETHING YOU DID, ANOTHER POSTCARD YOU LIKED, OR ANYTHING YOU BRAINSTORM!

IF YOU WANT, CUT IT OUT AND PUT IT IN AN ENVELOPE. MAIL IT, HAND DELIVER IT WHEN YOU RETURN HOME, OR KEEP IT IN YOUR JOURNAL.

ADVENTURE BINGO

FUNNY HAT	SELFIE STICK	FOOD ON A STICK	BIRD EATING	MOVING TRAIN
COIN ON THE GROUND	STRANGER BEING KIND	SOUVENIR POSTCARD	RED SHOES	BUS FILLED WITH TOURISTS
SOUVENIR SHOP	LEAF BIGGER THAN MY HAND	FREE	SOMEONE SPEAKING ANOTHER LANGUAGE	BOULDER BIGGER THAN ME
PERSON WITH A BACKPACK	PERSON WEARING PINK	PERSON CARRYING A BABY	PERSON WEARING A TIE	PERSON READING A TRAVEL GUIDE
PARADE OR FIREWORKS	CUP OF COFFEE	SOMEONE MY AGE	FOUR-LEGGED ANIMAL	REUSABLE WATER BOTTLE

TEAR THIS ONE OUT AND GIVE IT TO SOMEONE PLAY ALONG!
CAN THEY GET FIVE IN A ROW?

ADVENTURE BINGO

STRANGER BEING KIND	PERSON READING A TRAVEL GUIDE	SOUVENIR SHOP	BOULDER BIGGER THAN ME	BIRD EATING
SELFIE STICK	FOUR-LEGGED ANIMAL	SOUVENIR POSTCARD	PERSON WEARING A TIE	REUSABLE WATER BOTTLE
PERSON WITH A BACKPACK	LEAF BIGGER THAN MY HAND	FREE	FUNNY HAT	COIN ON THE GROUND
BUS FILLED WITH TOURISTS	PERSON CARRYING A BABY	MOVING TRAIN	PARADE OR FIREWORKS	SOMEONE SPEAKING ANOTHER LANGUAGE
CUP OF COFFEE	FOOD ON A STICK	SOMEONE MY AGE	PERSON WEARING PINK	RED SHOES

COLOR OR CROSS OFF EVERY DISCOVERY YOU MAKE.
CAN YOU GET FIVE IN A ROW?

DATE

INTERESTING THINGS I'VE SPIED

TODAY, I

SEE

HEAR

SMELL

TOUCH

TASTE

LAUGH

THINK

THIS INSIDE JOKE
MAKES ME BELLY-LAUGH!

THIS IS CRAZY!

THIS IS ME

GETTING SURPRISED

FEELING FABULOUS

LAUGHING

GETTING WET

RELAXING

WEARING A NEW

FUNNIEST MOMENT

COOLEST FIRST
EXPERIENCE

BEST MEMORY

WARMEST HUG

LONGEST DAY

MOST INCREDIBLE
SIGHT

PEOPLE I'VE MET

I THINK THIS PERSON IS

BECAUSE

I THINK THIS PERSON IS

BECAUSE

I THINK THIS PERSON IS

BECAUSE

I'M GOING TO MISS THIS

I ALWAYS WANT
TO REMEMBER THIS

HEADING HOME

HERE'S HOW I'M GETTING BACK HOME

THE FIRST THING I'M GOING TO DO THERE IS

I WON'T UNPACK ALL MY STUFF UNTIL

I'LL PROBABLY SLEEP _____ HOURS.

THE END. ALMOST.

I'M GLAD I KEPT THIS JOURNAL BECAUSE

I THINK I'LL STORE IT IN

IF ANYONE EVER ASKS ME FOR ADVICE ON HOW TO
KEEP A FANTASTIC TRAVEL JOURNAL, I'LL SAY

☐ THAT'S IT.
☐ WAIT! I STILL NEED TO ADD A FEW THINGS

☐ OKAY, I'M ALL DONE.
☐ ADVENTURE COMPLETE!

SHOW YOUR APPRECIATION

SURPRISE SOMEONE WITH GRATITUDE! CUT OUT THIS PAGE, DECORATE IT,
AND GIVE IT TO SOMEONE YOU ARE GRATEFUL FOR ON THIS TRIP.

THIS VACATION GRATITUDE AWARD
IS HEREBY GIVEN TO

ON THIS _____ **DAY OF** _____ , 20 _____

THANK YOU FOR MAKING MY VACATION SO

☐ RESTFUL   ☐ WELL ORGANIZED   ☐ EDUCATIONAL

☐ EXCITING   ☐ BEAUTIFUL   ☐ MEMORABLE

☐ ENTERTAINING   ☐ WILD   ☐

HERE'S YOU IN ACTION

BECAUSE OF YOU,

SIGNED WITH GRATITUDE BY